Living in Heaven's Blessings Now

Gloria Copeland

Harrison House
Tulsa, Oklahoma

Unless otherwise indicated, all Scripture quotations are taken from the *King James Version* of the Bible.

The Amplified Bible, Old Testament copyright © 1965, 1987 by the Zondervan Corporation. *The Amplifed Bible New Testament* copyright © 1954, 1958, 1987 by The Lockman Foundation. Used by permission.

Reprinted 2000   *3rd Printing*

Living in Heaven's Blessings Now
ISBN 1-57794-161-6
Copyright © 1998 by Gloria Copeland
Kenneth Copeland Ministries
Fort Worth, Texas 76192-0001

Published by Harrison House, Inc.
P.O. Box 35035
Tulsa, Oklahoma 74153

Printed in the United States of America. All rights reserved under International Copyright Law. Contents and/or cover may not be reproduced in whole or in part in any form without the express written consent of the Publisher.

Living in Heaven's Blessings Now

Where do you live?

I realize that's a simple question, but I want you to stop and think about your answer for a moment. Your immediate response might be to name a country or a city. You'd probably think of the spot on this earth where you wake up each morning and go to bed each night—the place where you keep your natural belongings.

But if you're a believer, you need to think more deeply than that.

You need to become aware of the fact that although you are in this world, you do not belong to this natural world's order. You are a citizen of heaven. You are, even here and now, privileged to live in that kingdom.

That statement would startle many Christians. Religion has taught them that they won't reach God's kingdom until they die and go to heaven. But the Bible says we've already made the transfer. It says, *"[The Father] has delivered and drawn us to Himself out of the control and the dominion of darkness and has transferred us into the kingdom of the Son of His love"* (Colossians 1:13, *The Amplified Bible*).

Because God dwells in us and among us, His kingdom is present with us right now. Jesus said it this way: *"...The kingdom of God does not come with signs to be observed or with visible display. Nor will people say, Look! Here [it is]! or, See, [it is] there! For behold, the kingdom of God is within you (in your hearts) and among you (surrounding you)"* (Luke 17:20-21, *The Amplified Bible*).

Certainly we will go on to the place called heaven when our bodies die or when Jesus catches us away. And that's great, because heaven is a wonderful place! It's the headquarters of this great kingdom. But, thank God, since we're already citizens of the kingdom now, we can enjoy many of the benefits of heaven right here on earth.

We can live our lives in love, peace, joy, prosperity, health and victory. We can also bring those kingdom blessings to others who are still under the dominion of darkness.

"If Christians can do that," you may ask, "why don't they?"

Mostly it's because they haven't been very aware of the kingdom of God. They have been so absorbed in the kingdom of this world—the world that they can see and touch—they haven't given much thought to God's kingdom. They've gotten so caught up in the "busyness" of this natural world and its demands, so familiar with its way of operating, that they're practically strangers to the operations of the kingdom of God.

But we can change that, in the Name of Jesus! We can obey the instruction of the Apostle Paul who wrote: "...*aim at and seek the [rich, eternal treasures] that are above, where Christ [the Anointed One] is, seated at the right hand of God. And set your minds and keep them set on what is above—the higher things—not on the things that are on the earth"* (Colossians 3:1-2, *The Amplified Bible*).

By studying and meditating on what the Word has to say about the kingdom of God, we can become more and more kingdom-of-God minded. There is so much information in the Word about the kingdom of God, I could talk about it for hours—and I have. Brother Jesse Duplantis says Ken and I are the only preachers he knows who can preach on the same sermon for a year. But we can't help it! That's how long it takes us to get through!

So all I can do in this book is get you started. I challenge you to take up this study on your own from here. Get out your concordance and look up all the references to the *kingdom of God* or the *kingdom of heaven.* I believe the New Testament uses them interchangeably. Let the reality of that kingdom get down in your heart so that you are aware of it every day.

A Superior Kingdom

The first important truth the Word reveals about the kingdom of God is that it is sovereign, or superior, to all other kingdoms. It is chief, the greatest, the most supreme in power, rank and authority.

Actually, the very word *kingdom* comes from the joining of two other words: *king* and *dominion*. A kingdom is the place where the king has dominion. Therefore, the kingdom of God is where God has dominion.

Since God owns everything in heaven and in earth, He could take dominion everywhere. But He has chosen to exercise that dominion through man. He gave Adam authority over the earth in the Garden of Eden. That's why Jesus had to come into the earth and become flesh. To exercise God's dominion over Satan in the earth, He had to do it as a man.

The second important truth the Word reveals about the kingdom of God is the one we've already mentioned: The kingdom of God is present here and now. It occupies the same space this natural world occupies. You may not be able to see it, but it is here and very real, nevertheless.

I think one of the best illustrations of that fact is found in 2 Kings 6, where the prophet Elisha and his servant were surrounded by a great army sent to take them captive:

...Elisha's servant said to him, Alas, my master! What shall we do? Elisha answered, Fear not;

for those with us are more than those with them. Then Elisha prayed, Lord, I pray You, open his eyes that he may see. And the Lord opened the young man's eyes, and he saw; and behold, the mountain was full of horses and chariots of fire round about Elisha (verses 15-17, *The Amplified Bible*).

Those angelic horses and chariots were there to protect Elisha and his servant the whole time—even though most of that time they were not visible to the natural eye. The angels occupied the same space the enemy army occupied. Since the angels were from a superior kingdom, Elisha wasn't afraid. He knew God's kingdom would prevail.

If you'll just grasp that one fact, it will enable you to walk in great joy and peace in the midst of this messed-up world. If you'll just realize the kingdom of God has dominion and control over the natural realm, then you won't be afraid. You can rejoice knowing that because you belong to God's kingdom, you can take dominion over every natural circumstance the devil tries to use against you.

Glory to God! Isn't that thrilling?

A Ministry of Heavenly Breakthroughs

Of course, Jesus is the One Who made that possible for us. He opened the way. He established God's kingdom among us and showed us how to bring it into manifestation in this natural world.

"But Gloria," you may say, "I thought Jesus said His kingdom wasn't of this world."

He did, but that doesn't mean His kingdom doesn't operate in this world. It means that its power didn't originate here. *The Amplified Bible* says it this way, *"...My kingdom is not from [this world]—has no such origin or source"* (John 18:36).

Jesus' whole ministry was one of preaching and demonstrating the kingdom of God. As Mark 1:14-15 says, His ministry began when He *"came into Galilee, preaching the gospel of the kingdom of God, And saying, The time is fulfilled, and the kingdom of God is at hand: repent ye, and believe the gospel."*

Jesus was saying, "You don't have to wait anymore. The dominion of God, His kingdom, is here right now! You can come in. God's power is here to break into this natural world and to heal, deliver and set you free! So change your mind. Quit thinking like you used to think. Believe this good news!"

Luke 4 spells that message out even more clearly. It tells how Jesus stood in the synagogue and preached from Isaiah 61, saying:

The Spirit of the Lord [is] upon Me, because He has anointed Me...to preach the good news (the Gospel) to the poor; He has sent Me to announce release to the captives, and recovery of sight to the blind; to send forth delivered those who are oppressed—who are downtrodden, bruised, crushed and broken down by calamity; To proclaim the accepted and acceptable year of the Lord— the day when salvation and the free favors of God profusely abound...Today this Scripture has been fulfilled while you are

present and hearing (Luke 4:18-19, 21, *The Amplified Bible*).

Jesus said, "I am anointed." What is the anointing? It's the manifestation of God's presence that brings deliverance. The anointing is the kingdom of God bursting in upon this natural realm and bringing God's free favors profusely. Profusely means *lavishly, liberally, extravagantly, over and abounding.* Hallelujah!

Jesus didn't just preach about this divine kingdom. He demonstrated it. He operated in the dominion of God by taking authority over the evil spirits that had bound people, and by laying hands on the sick and driving out sickness from their bodies.

Read through the Gospels and see for yourself. Time after time, Jesus exercised the dominion of the kingdom of God. He came to Peter's house, found Peter's mother-in-law sick, laid His hands on her and healed her.

The leper came to Him for healing and He said, *"Be thou clean,"* and immediately the leprosy was cleansed. Jairus' daughter died, and Jesus raised her from the dead. He cast the demons out of the madman of Gadara. When there wasn't enough food to feed the thousands who were listening to Him preach in a remote place, He multiplied a few loaves and fish into more than enough food to feed the whole crowd!

Do you know what those instances were? They were times when the kingdom of God broke through into this natural realm by the anointing that was on Jesus. They were heavenly breakthroughs!

Take Off the Limits

Jesus didn't intend for those break-throughs to stop at the end of His earthly ministry, either. He commissioned His disciples to continue His ministry. He told us to go about healing the sick and bringing other heavenly breakthroughs, saying, *"...The kingdom of God has come close to you"* (Luke 10:9, *The Amplified Bible*).

Jesus commanded us to:

...Go ye into all the world, and preach the gospel *[the good news that the kingdom of God is here]* **to every creature. He that believeth and is baptized shall be saved; but he that believeth not shall be damned. And these signs** *[or heavenly breakthroughs]* **shall follow them that believe; In my name shall they cast out devils; they**

shall speak with new tongues; They shall take up serpents; and if they drink any deadly thing, it shall not hurt them; they shall lay hands on the sick, and they shall recover (Mark 16:15-18).

It's the responsibility of the Church to manifest the kingdom of God in this natural realm. It's our job to exercise the dominion of that kingdom, and demonstrate it so others can experience the reality of it and become citizens of God's kingdom themselves!

Until now, the Church hasn't been getting that job done nearly as well as it should. Why is that? Primarily, it's because most believers have become so busy with the natural affairs of life, they haven't had time to learn much about how to operate in the kingdom of God.

They're so busy seeking the things of this world—food, clothes, houses, cars, money to pay their bills—they don't even give much thought to the things of God's kingdom.

Actually, that's not very smart. Why should we invest ourselves so much in this natural world? Its systems are limited. When we face impossible situations, this natural world has no answer for us. It cannot help us with an incurable disease or an insoluble financial crisis.

But with God all things are possible! There are no limitations in the kingdom of God! It knows no impossibilities! So what we need to do is to obey the instructions Jesus gave in Matthew 6:

...Take no thought for your life, what ye shall eat, or what ye shall drink; nor yet for your

body, what ye shall put on... (For after all these things do the Gentiles seek:) for your heavenly Father knoweth that ye have need of these things. But seek ye first the kingdom of God, and his righteousness; and all these things shall be added unto you (verses 25, 32-33).

The Amplified Bible clarifies that last verse even more. It says, *"...seek for (aim at and strive after) first of all His kingdom, and His righteousness [His way of doing and being right]...."* In other words, if we want to operate in the dominion of God, we have to find out His way of doing things and then do things His way. We'll have to change the way we think. We'll have to start thinking and acting like He does instead of thinking and acting like the world does.

We'll have to seek Him and His principles, put our dependence first and foremost on Him, and then He'll see to it that our natural needs are met.

You see, the principles of the kingdom of God always work. God has spoken and set them into motion by His Word. They will work for anyone who will put them to work.

For example, one of those principles, the primary one, is the law of sowing and reaping. Galatians 6:7-8 states that law very simply: *"Be not deceived; God is not mocked: for whatsoever a man soweth, that shall he also reap. For he that soweth to his flesh shall of the flesh reap corruption; but he that soweth to the Spirit shall of the Spirit reap life everlasting."*

Actually, the law of sowing and reaping works in both the kingdom of

God and the kingdom of this world. If you sow into the kingdom of darkness, you reap the harvest of that kingdom, which is death in all its forms. If you invest your time and money in the concerns of the world, you'll end up on drugs, pornography and alcohol. You'll end up sick and unhappy.

On the other hand, if you sow to the kingdom of God, you'll reap the harvest of that kingdom. If you invest yourself in the affairs of God, you'll end up with abundant life in all its forms. As Romans 8:6 says, *"For to be carnally minded [to think like the world thinks] is death; but to be spiritually minded [to think like God thinks] is life and peace."*

It's Up to You

Of course, if you want to sow to the kingdom of God you must first be born again. You do that simply by making Jesus the Lord of your life.

You can read the Bible all day, and it won't make sense to you if you haven't taken that first step. The great kingdom truths it contains will be hidden from you. Why? Because, as Jesus said, *"...Except a man be born again, he cannot see the kingdom of God"* (John 3:3).

A person who hasn't been born again simply cannot understand the way God thinks. The ways of His kingdom are beyond his grasp because he is in darkness.

When you've been born again, however, you are translated into God's kingdom. You immediately have the ability to know and walk in God's ways. How much you do from then on is up to you. The more you seek after God and His way of doing and being right, the more of His power and dominion you'll enjoy. The more you renew your mind to His Word—which is His way of thinking—and change your life in obedience to that Word, the more you'll see the kingdom of heaven manifested in your life and in the lives of those around you.

The wonderful thing about the kingdom of God is that you don't have to be rich or smart or talented to walk in it. Anyone can do it. All you have to do is find out what God says and act on it. When you do that, blessings—heavenly breakthroughs—will begin to happen.

So I want to encourage you to start today investing more of yourself, more of your time, thought and energy, into seeking the kingdom of God. Determine in your heart to change some areas in your life, to dig into the Word more deeply and find out what God says about those areas. Then start acting like He does instead of like the world.

Heighten your awareness of the kingdom of God. Get more and more kingdom-of-God minded. Then get ready for the blessings of heaven—the lavish, liberal-to-excess, extravagant and over-abounding favors of the kingdom of God—to break through on you!

Prayer for Salvation
and Baptism in the Holy Spirit

Heavenly Father, I come to You in the Name of Jesus. Your Word says, *"Whosoever shall call on the name of the Lord shall be saved"* (Acts 2:21). I am calling on You. I pray and ask Jesus to come into my heart and be Lord over my life, according to Romans 10:9-10: *"If thou shalt confess with thy mouth the Lord Jesus, and shalt believe in thine heart that God hath raised him from the dead, thou shalt be saved. For with the heart man believeth unto righteousness; and with the mouth confession is made unto salvation."* I do that now. I confess that Jesus is Lord, and I believe in my heart that God raised Him from the dead.

I am now reborn! I am a Christian—a child of Almighty God! I am saved! You also said in Your Word, *"If ye then, being evil, know how to give good gifts unto your children: HOW MUCH MORE shall your heavenly Father give the Holy Spirit to them that ask him?"* (Luke 11:13). I'm also asking You to fill me with the Holy Spirit. Holy Spirit, rise up within me as I praise God. I fully expect to speak with other tongues as You give me utterance (Acts 2:4).

Begin to praise God for filling you with the Holy Spirit. Speak those words and syllables you receive—not in your own language, but the language given to you by the Holy Spirit. You have to use your own voice. God will not force you to speak. Worship and praise Him in your heavenly language—in other tongues.

Continue with the blessing God has given you and pray in tongues each day.

You are a born-again, Spirit-filled believer. You'll never be the same!

Find a good Word of God preaching church, and become a part of a church family who will love and care for you as you love and care for them.

We need to be connected to each other. It increases our strength in God. It's God's plan for us.

About the Author

Together with her husband, Kenneth, Gloria Copeland's impact on the kingdom of God has been felt worldwide. She teaches around the world on God's will for healing and divine health, His plan for prosperity, His great plan for man's salvation and more. With an anointing for powerful preaching and the compassion of Jesus for the sick, Gloria moves and ministers in the Spirit of God. Recipient of the Christian Woman of the Year Award, her book Hidden Treasures was recently number 16 on the Christian Booksellers Association list.

Books Available from Kenneth Copeland Ministries

by Kenneth Copeland

* A Ceremony of Marriage
  A Matter of Choice
  Covenant of Blood
  Faith and Patience—The Power Twins
* Freedom From Fear
  Giving and Receiving
  Honor—Walking in Honesty, Truth and Integrity
  How to Conquer Strife
  How to Discipline Your Flesh
  How to Receive Communion
  Living at the End of Time—A Time of Supernatural Increase
  Love Never Fails
  Managing God's Mutual Funds
* Now Are We in Christ Jesus
* Our Covenant With God
* Prayer—Your Foundation for Success
* Prosperity: The Choice Is Yours
  Rumors of War
* Sensitivity of Heart
* Six Steps to Excellence in Ministry
  Sorrow Not! Winning Over Grief and Sorrow
* The Decision Is Yours
* The Force of Faith
* The Force of Righteousness
  The Image of God in You
  The Laws of Prosperity
* The Mercy of God
  The Miraculous Realm of God's Love
  The Outpouring of the Spirit—The Result of Prayer
* The Power of the Tongue
  The Power to Be Forever Free
  The Troublemaker
* The Winning Attitude
  Turn Your Hurts Into Harvests
* Welcome to the Family
* You Are Healed!
  Your Right-Standing With God

by Gloria Copeland

* And Jesus Healed Them All
  Are You Listening?
  Are You Ready?
  Build Your Financial Foundation
  Build Yourself an Ark
  Fight On!
  God's Prescription for Divine Health
  God's Success Formula
  God's Will for You
  God's Will for Your Healing
  God's Will is Prosperity
* God's Will Is the Holy Spirit
* Harvest of Health
  Hidden Treasures
  Living Contact

Living in Heaven's Blessings Now
* Love—The Secret to Your Success
No Deposit—No Return
Pleasing the Father
Pressing In—It's Worth It All
Shine On!
The Power to Live a New Life
The Unbeatable Spirit of Faith
This Same Jesus
* Walk in the Spirit
Walk With God
Well Worth the Wait

Books Co-Authored by Kenneth and Gloria Copeland
Family Promises
Healing Promises
Prosperity Promises
Protection Promises

* From Faith to Faith—A Daily Guide to Victory
From Faith to Faith—A Perpetual Calendar

One Word From God Series
• One Word from God Can Change Your Destiny
• One Word from God Can Change Your Family
• One Word from God Can Change Your Finances
• One Word From God Can Change Your Formula for Success
• One Word from God Can Change Your Health
• One Word From God Can Change Your Nation
• One Word From God Can Change Your Prayer Life
• One Word From God Can Change Your Relationships

Over the Edge—A Youth Devotional
Over the Edge Xtreme Planner for Students—
  Designed for the School Year

Pursuit of His Presence—A Daily Devotional
Pursuit of His Presence—A Perpetual Calendar

Other Books Published by KCP
The First 30 Years—A Journey of Faith
  The story of the lives of Kenneth and Gloria Copeland
Real People. Real Needs. Real Victories.
  A book of testimonies to encourage your faith.

John G. Lake—His Life, His Sermons, His Boldness of Faith
The Holiest of All, by Andrew Murray
The New Testament in Modern Speech, by Richard Francis Weymouth

Products Designed for Today's Children and Youth
Baby Praise Board Book
Baby Praise Christmas Board Book
Noah's Ark Coloring Book
Shout! Super-Activity Book

Commander Kellie and the Superkids Adventure Novels
#1 The Mysterious Presence
#2 The Quest for the Second Half
#3 Escape From Jungle Island
#4 In Pursuit of the Enemy

SWORD Adventure Book

*Available in Spanish

World Offices
of Kenneth Copeland Ministries

For more information and a free catalog,
please write the office nearest you.

Kenneth Copeland Ministries
Fort Worth, Texas 76192-0001

Kenneth Copeland
Locked Bag 2600
Mansfield Delivery Centre
QUEENSLAND 4122
AUSTRALIA

Kenneth Copeland
Post Office Box 15
BATH
BA1 1GD
ENGLAND U.K.

Kenneth Copeland
Private Bag X 909
FONTAINEBLEAU 2032
REPUBLIC OF SOUTH AFRICA

Kenneth Copeland
Post Office Box 378
SURREY, BC V3T 5B6
CANADA

UKRAINE
L'VIV 290000
Post Office Box 84
Kenneth Copeland
L'VIV 290000
UKRAINE

Learn more about Kenneth Copeland Ministries
by visiting our website at:
www.kcm.org

We're Here for You!

Believer's Voice of Victory Television Broadcast

Join Kenneth and Gloria Copeland and the *Believer's Voice of Victory* broadcasts Monday through Friday and on Sunday each week, and learn how faith in God's Word can take your life from ordinary to extraordinary. This teaching from God's Word is designed to get you where you want to be—*on top!*

You can catch the *Believer's Voice of Victory* broadcast on your local, cable or satellite channels.

*Check your local listings for times and stations in your area.

Believer's Voice of Victory Magazine

Enjoy inspired teaching and encouragement from Kenneth and Gloria Copeland and guest ministers each month in the *Believer's Voice of Victory* magazine. Also included are real-life testimonies of God's miraculous power and divine intervention into the lives of people just like you!

It's more than just a magazine-it's a ministry.

Shout! ...The dynamic magazine just for kids!

Shout! The Voice of Victory for Kids is a Bible-charged, action-packed, bimonthly magazine available FREE to kids everywhere! Featuring Wichita Slim and Commander Kellie and the Superkids, *Shout!* is filled with colorful adventure comics, challenging games and puzzles, exciting short stories, solve-it-yourself mysteries and much more!!

Stand up, sign up and get ready to Shout!

To receive a FREE subscription to *Believer's Voice of Victory,* or to give a child you know a FREE subscription to *Shout!,* write:

Kenneth Copeland Ministries
Fort Worth, Texas 76192-0001
or call:
1-800-600-7395
(9 a.m.-5 p.m. CT)
Or visit our website at:
www.kcm.org

If you are writing from outside the U.S., please contact the KCM office nearest you. Addresses for all Kenneth Copeland Ministries offices are listed on the previous page.

The Harrison House Vision

Proclaiming the truth and the power
Of the Gospel of Jesus Christ
With excellence;

Challenging Christians to
Live victoriously,
Grow spiritually,
Know God intimately.